TURNING BO:
WITH THREADED LIDS

Bill Bowers

Schiffer Publishing Ltd ®

4880 Lower Valley Road, Atglen, Pennsylvania 19310

Dedication

To: Susan, my soul mate, life long companion, and best friend.

Contents

Other Schiffer Books by Bill Bowers:

The Basics of Turning Spirals,
ISBN: 0-7643-2592-2, $14.95

10 Easy Turning Projects for the Smaller Lathe,
ISBN: 978-0-7643-2727-8, $14.95

7 Great Turning Projects for the Smaller Lathe,
ISBN: 978-0-7643-2726-1, $14.95

Turning Boxes with Friction-Fitted Lids,
ISBN: 978-0-7643-3027-8

Designed by Stephanie Daugherty
Type set in BauerBodni BdCn BT/Zurich BT

ISBN: 978-0-7643-3131-2
Printed in China

Schiffer Books are available at special discounts for bulk purchases for sales promotions or premiums. Special editions, including personalized covers, corporate imprints, and excerpts can be created in large quantities for special needs. For more information contact the publisher:

Published by Schiffer Publishing Ltd.
4880 Lower Valley Road
Atglen, PA 19310
Phone: (610) 593-1777; Fax: (610) 593-2002
E-mail: Info@schifferbooks.com

For the largest selection of fine reference books on this and related subjects, please visit our web site at **www.schifferbooks.com**
We are always looking for people to write books on new and related subjects. If you have an idea for a book please contact us at the above address.

This book may be purchased from the publisher.
Include $5.00 for shipping.
Please try your bookstore first.
You may write for a free catalog.

In Europe, Schiffer books are distributed by
Bushwood Books
6 Marksbury Ave.
Kew Gardens
Surrey TW9 4JF England
Phone: 44 (0) 20 8392-8585;
Fax: 44 (0) 20 8392-9876
E-mail: info@bushwoodbooks.co.uk
Website: www.bushwoodbooks.co.uk
Free postage in the U.K., Europe; air mail at cost.

Proem

Although this well illustrated, caption driven instructional text is yet another amongst the multitude of books, VHS tapes, and DVDs produced on how to turn boxes, it is truly unique as to the ingenious quality of projects described. Firstly, the boxes all have hand thread-chased fitted lids. This technique solves the fitting problems experienced whenever producing boxes in a damp climate to be shipped to a dry climate and vice versa. Secondly, each chapter uniquely describes differing as well as divergent approaches to turned boxes and how to chase threads in differing circumstances. Various boxes that one may never have seen are explained in detail allowing one to easily turn them to completion. Thirdly, most projects save for the first two display the use of a rose engine lathe to decorate, embellish, and enhance the appearances of the various boxes.

As with many texts on turning boxes, the ideas are not original but borrowed from master turners with additional steps and procedures added to improve and personalize the structures.

• Chapter one describes how to make use of left-over glued timber from peppermill stocks to construct attractive cylinder boxes. The technique of using dyed epoxy for hand thread-chasing proposed by Petter Herud is explained and demonstrated in detail.

• Chapter two explains how to construct the cubic box with a pyramidal threaded lid. A second technique using boxwood sleeves to construct a threaded fitted lid is described. A similar non-threaded box has oft times been demonstrated by Clead Christiansen at symposiums.

• Chapter three reveals the secrets of making spherical boxes that were made popular by Stuart Batty and further extended by Christian Dehlon. A third technique of using cyanoacrylate treated wood to chase threads is demonstrated. By embellishing the finished product with rose engine lathe work and hand thread-chasing the fit a rather individualistic keepsake is created. Ornamental stands out of exotics are created to display the unusual boxes.

• Chapter four reveals a take-off of Hans Weissflog's rotating ringed lidded boxes with threaded lids and rose engine lathe decorations.

• Chapter five discusses the bolt boxes first popularized by Allan Batty, then extended by Petter Herud. These have been further improved upon by rose engine lathe embellishments.

• Chapter six describes another of Hans Weissflog's creations, the pierced-though lid. The lid is thread-chased, the box bottom decorated ornamentally inside and out, and then some lids inlaid with contrasting timbers as accents on their undersides. The pierced-through procedure is further modified by using an eccentric chuck to individualize the design.

• The final chapter, seven, is a compendium of various threaded boxes to entice the reader to try his/her own accents and personalization at improving the age old boxes.

One may start anywhere in the book to create their project or work through from the beginning towards the end. Reasonably good skill at turning and tooling are required to produce the end product. Standard turning tools are required with some special tools described in the individual chapters. One need not own a large lathe to create the boxes, but a lathe with adjustable slow speeds is necessary to adequately thread-chase and an indexing system is helpful for some of the projects. Construction of a rose engine lathe is necessary to produce the ornamental designs. Even though it may be time consuming, the effort is well worth the time invested. A visit to ornamentalturning.org on the web will yield more information on rose engine lathes, their construction, and outlets to purchase kits, parts, pieces, as well as finished lathes.

One may try their hand at any of the detailed described projects to gain considerable satisfaction and accomplishment upon completion. Remember to have fun and pass on to others knowledge gained at the lathe.

Chapter 1
Cylinder Boxes with Dyed Epoxy Threads

There is a multitude of procedures to hand chase threads for lidded boxes, but I am aware of only four. The first, described in this chapter, utilizes aniline dyed, slow curing epoxy. The reasons for using slow curing epoxy become evident whenever one uses the fast set brands. If the epoxy sets too fast it tends to be somewhat crystallized and brittle; consequently, it may fracture when being turned. The slow set epoxies tend to be more pliable even though they are hard. Turning the slow cured epoxy will peel off long strips of impressive ribbons as the epoxy is heated under the pressure of the turning tool.

The amount of dye added depends upon how deeply colored one wishes the epoxy to be. A washed out color is displeasing to the artistic eye, so enough dye needs to be added to give an opaque appearance of intense color. One critical fact to remember is not to add too much water or non-epoxy material, because the epoxy will never cure. A gooey mess will ensue making it impossible to chase threads and it will gum up tools, lathe beds, walls, clothes, or anything else that happens to be in the path of the dyed epoxy air-born globs (my shop still has dyed epoxy spattered from earlier experiments).

One must be careful using aniline dye powders as aniline is a toxic substance. Always wear a dust mask, gloves, and protective clothing whenever using the powder. Once it is mixed with water or alcohol the risk drops considerably. A small amount of powder in water stirred to the proper mixture will give the necessary concentrated color. Use only a few drops in the mixed epoxy (parts A and B in proportions suggested by the manufacture) to get a deep pigmented effect. The powder could be added directly, but I find premixing pigments more convenient and easier to judge proper amounts for coloring. Some manufacturers make a pigmented epoxy concentrate to add to the clear epoxy but there usually aren't many available colors. Sometimes a few drops of acrylic dye may be utilized for coloring.

The next step to ponder is allowing the dyed epoxy enough time to cure or set before turning. A conservative estimate is 72 hours. Often times the epoxy will contract making a meniscus in the cut rebate. This will necessitate another application of the same colored epoxy—a good reason to record how much dye and the quantity of epoxy utilized initially—so that a full-thickness thread may be created. One must then allow another 72 hours of curing before turning the dyed epoxy.

By now some may be wondering why one would use epoxy for threads in the first place. The answer is simply that some woods which may be highly figured and conducive to box making are too soft or brittle to hold threads. Sometimes odd angled glue-ups or segmented structures make lovely boxes but can't be threaded. Epoxy may be poured into a turned rebate of almost any wood or turnable material even MDF.

The first time I saw epoxy used for threads was whenever Petter Herud demonstrated the technique at our association's annual wood turning symposium and master classes. His signature techniques are what this chapter describes.

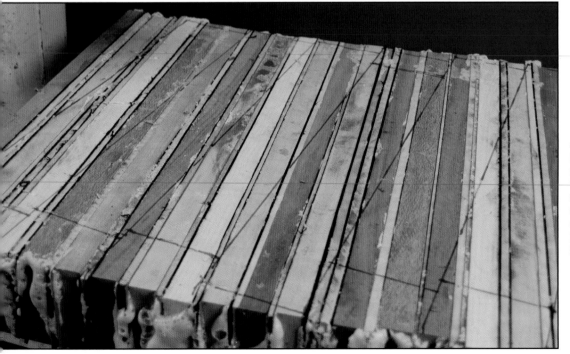

After making 15-inch tall peppermills from various glued-up timbers and cutting them on the bias there are a number of left over blocks at the ends, as noted on the drawn green cut lines. They measure approximately 3 x 3 x 1-1/2 inches.

The side view of glued-up end pieces displays an interesting pattern to be utilized in boxes.

Use the narrow parting tool (1/16-inch) to cut into the stock leaving a 1/2-inch dowel.

Cut two short blocks with a chop saw. Glue sandwiched veneer between the two pieces, and square the ends with a chop saw. The stock is, then mounted between centers and turned to a cylinder. Turn a 1-1/2-inch diameter, 1/8-inch wide spigot at both squared ends, and mount the cylinder in the O'Donnell jaws.

Draw a red pencil line about 2/5 of the way down from the tailstock end (this approximates the golden mean—phi= 1.6180339887, a number that goes to infinity without repeating and the usual ratio used in art, architecture, or other visual presentations—for correct proportions). The shorter portion will be the lid and the longer is the base.

Remove the tailstock and cut through the dowel, grasping the lid before it hits the floor.

The pattern of the cut surface is demonstrated on the underside of the lid.

On a 1/4-inch bar of high speed steel mounted in a handle, fashion a rebate cutter by grinding a curved bevel (40 degree angle) at the tip and a 60 degree bevel on the left side—the side in contact with the stock—about 5/8 inch from the tip.

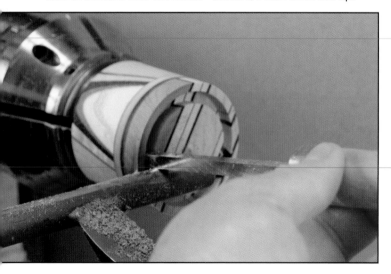

Cut a 1/4-inch deep, 1/4-inch wide rebate in the top of the base. It should be 1/8 to 3/16 inches from the outside edge of the cylinder. Make sure to cut at an angle as demonstrated and use a light touch because the rebate cutter is quite aggressive.

Remove the base and mount the lid to make a similar rebate cut. Remember to mark top and bottom with letters or numbers so the parts don't get mixed up with other stock during gluing.

The rebates on the base and lid are filled with a two-part, slow curing epoxy. A few drops of aniline dye can be added to produce the desired color. Carefully pour the mixture into the rebate. Notice there is some spill over on the surface which will allow for the shrinkage and prohibit most menisci formation. Don't let any epoxy run down the sides.

Note: Porous timbers are not good to use for this technique as the epoxy will wick through and dye the wood. With non-dyed epoxy, this property could be of some advantage should one wish to strengthen timber for other purposes. On the other hand, several coats of 1-1/2 lb. cut blond shellac in the rebate may partially seal some porous timbers.

After the epoxy has cured 72 hours and the menisci have been filled in with an additional application of epoxy, remount the lid for turning.

True the surface with the 3/8-inch spindle gouge.

Remember to begin drilling at dead center with a closed flute and sweep out to the periphery leaving a wall thickness of about 1/4-inch.

In preparation for hollowing the lid, set a depth gauge to 1/4 inch less than the depth of the lid. This 1/4 inch will be the thickness of the lid top.

Use the depth gauge to check for proper thickness of the lid top.

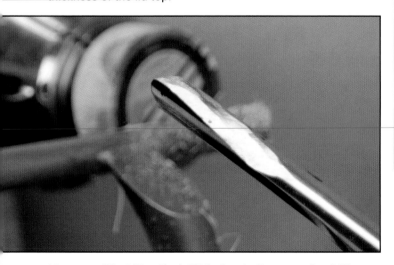

Use a modified (Ray Key) 1/2-inch spindle gouge for drilling and hollowing the lid.

Use a round-edged square nose scraper to smooth out the inside of the lid, making the inside base of the lid subtlety curved to the smooth sides. Next use the rebate tool to cut a 3/8-inch deep, 1/8-inch wide shelf in the epoxy for thread chasing. This shelf is cut so that the interior of the lid and base will have a smooth continuous line without a step being formed. The step of the lid will fit the reverse step of the base giving the smooth transition.

A tool needs to be fashioned to cut a slight rebate or groove beyond the epoxy. The rebate should be 1/8-inch wide and about 1/16-inch deep. It will serve as a stop-gap when chasing the threads so that the thread chasing tool may be withdrawn prior to fouling on the lid's interior. The tool shown was ground from a worn out high speed steel tool.

In the underside of the lid you can turn concentric circles with the skew tip for a design element. Finish the interior lid by sanding with waxed sandpaper, moving from 150-400 grits and reversing lathe directions between grits, followed by waxed #0000 steel wool. Apply diluted lacquer (1/2 Deft plus 1/2 lacquer thinner). Friction dry with a clean cloth and then apply Briwax and polish.

The 1/8-inch wide, 1/16-inch deep rebate cut beyond the green epoxy.

Hand Thread Chasing

Before going any further, some words need to be said about hand thread chasing. Before the advent of cyanoacrylate and other acceptable glues, threads were extensively used by master turners to screw together assorted pieces. The technique may be likened to riding a bicycle or driving a car. One may read extensively about it or observe a person doing it, but until the individual actually accomplishes the task it can't be mastered. Consequently, narratives, DVD's or videos are poor seconds to hands-on experience.

There are two types of thread chasers, male and female. Both require some grinding to become functional. The female thread chaser shown in the next photo has had its right side ground to a taper to fit into narrowed areas and the top formed by a hollow grind. Never, never, never grind the teeth except to knock off a bit of the first tooth's bottom on each side of the male thread chaser. A hollow grind on its top is also necessary.

Thread chasers come in various sizes—threads per inch or "tpi." The finer threads, such as 20 tpi, are easier to use, especially in greasy timbers such as cocobolo, blackwood, boxwood, or lignum vitae. Some of the more brittle exotics will chase better with coarser threads, such as 16 tpi. Some threads, such as 10 or 12 tpi, are difficult to form in nearly any wood. Synthetic substances, such as epoxies or imitation ivory, chase well with nearly any chaser.

The female thread chaser used on the green dyed epoxy is a 20 tpi tool.

After some threads begin to be cut, straighten the chaser and continue cutting to the stop-gap. The chaser will be automatically pulled in by the threads. Remember to pull away from the side when the rebate is reached or the tool will foul on the blunt spigot and strip the threads. Repeat the process several times to deepen the cut and threads.

After the threads are adequately chased as deeply as you desire, apply wax with a hard or stiff toothbrush (most difficult to find these days), preferable one dedicated to this purpose.

Begin with subtle chamfer cut at the epoxy's edge, formed by holding the thread chaser at 45 degrees with the lathe running at 300 rpms. If one's lathe can't be slowed to 200 and 300 rpms, threads can't be chased.

The finished interior and threads are ready to be placed on the box's base.

Remove the lid and mount the base in the O'Donnell jaws.

Cut a narrow spigot to the marked line and check to make sure it is proud of the threaded epoxy sleeve in the lid.

Square the surface with the 3/8-inch spindle gouge, then set the dividers slightly proud of the interior diameter of the lid's epoxy threads, and mark it on the epoxy ring of the base.

After reaching the proper diameter, extend the spigot to the entire width of the green-dyed epoxy. Notice the fine ribbons from the cut epoxy.

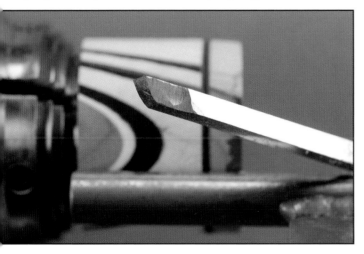

For the epoxy spigot, use the same rebate tool as was used for cutting the original epoxy rebate slots.

Using the narrow parting tool cut a 1/16-inch deep, 1/16-inch wide slot at the base of the spigot to act as a stop-gap for withdrawing the male chaser when making the threads.

Notice how a hollow grind has been applied to the top of the male thread chaser and the lower sharp teeth at the bottom edges have been slightly rounded.

Start at the edge with a 45 degree angle, then make rotating circular, counterclockwise motions to begin to cut threads at 200 rpms. If the lathe speed is too slow, a wavy or drunken thread will result.

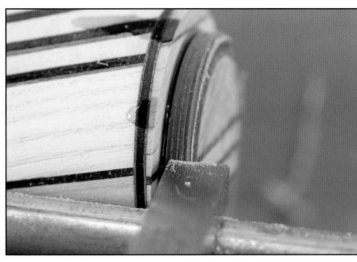

Continue to run the chaser towards the headstock cutting threads and withdrawing when you reach cut stop-gap.

After adequate threads are produced check the fit of the lid. It is best if only about 3 threads are turned to fit the lid, so the lid can be removed easily and quickly. Another technique is to place a slight taper to the threads so that only a 90 or 180 degree turn is necessary for a tight fit.

Check the fit of the lid to assure that it is tight. At this juncture some material may be removed from the top of the male-threaded spigot to make a proper alignment of lid to base, though it might be difficult to tell which is what with such a complicated design.

Remove the lid and cut a 1/32-inch wide, 1/32-inch deep defining mark between the base and lid. Replace the lid.

Use a skew to smooth any circumferential irregularities.

Use the tip of the skew to cut concentric rings into the top of the lid for a design.

Finish the outside top and sides of the box by sanding with waxed sandpaper, ranging from 150-400 grits, reversing directions between grits. Buff with waxed #0000 steel wool, apply diluted lacquer, friction dried, and then buff with Briwax.

Using a 3/8-inch spindle gouge remove the spigot from the lid's top and smooth out the surface.

Remove the lid to hollow the base with the modified spindle gouge that was used for the lid.

Finish the interior by sanding, applying friction dried lacquer, and buffing with Briwax. Remember to finish the interior spigot but not the threads.

Check the depth to assure a 1/4-inch thickness of the bottom.

Remove the base and place a scrap piece in the O'Donnell jaws with a spigot cut to firmly fit the opening of the box.

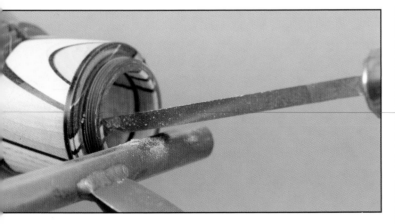

Use a rounded-corner square-nose scrapper to smooth the bottom and side walls of the interior. Remember to apply the scrapper with the proper angle, as shown, to prevent nasty catches. Turn some concentric circles on the bottom for design.

Mount the base and turn off its spigot with the 3/8-inch spindle gouge.

Turn the bottom to completion, placing concentric circles with the skew for design. Sand, lacquer, then wax.

Left: The finished top and bottom present an attractive box.

Bottom Left: The finished interior of top and bottom are as attractive as well.

Below: The completed box will make a conversation piece no matter what or where its use may be.

Chapter 2
Cubic Boxes with Threaded Pyramidal Lids

Several years ago, I remember watching Clead Christiansen demonstrate how to turn a cubic box at the Provo Woodturning Symposium in Utah. He had stated someone else had the original idea but the process intrigued me enough that it should be displayed here with some additions and modifications.

A cubic box with a spherical interior and a 3-prong turned foot with a screw-on contrasting pyramidal lid makes a fascinating gallery type piece and a challenging engineering project.

The problem is holding the cube between centers safely to turn off the pointed tip and hollow out the interior without going through the sides or bottom. This requires the jig shown below.

To make a jig, two pieces of 5/8-inch plywood are cut to 9-inch discs and turned true on the lathe. A 3-inch diameter piece of 3/4-inch Baltic birch plywood is turned true then glued to the center of one disc for the bottom of the jig. The top portion of the jig then has a 3-inch diameter tapered hole turned so that the three sides of the cube can be held at three points, defining the top plane of the portion to be removed. The bottom of the jig is mounted in #3 Talon Oneway jaws and a cone to fit the bottom pyramidal area of the box is turned. Six 3/4-inch screws are then used to fix the base plate to the jig's bottom—glue is not sufficiently strong to hold the base plate when applying tremendous torque created while hollowing the cube.

Using the lathe's indexing system drill a hole at each 90 degree point to hold the bolts that will secure the cubic stock in the jig.

The 3-1/2-inch cube of maple burl, which as been accurately cut with the band saw, is placed, point-first, between the jig's bottom and a Oneway live cup center to assure a "square" fit. Note that the top portion of the jig must be placed over the live center before the cube is centered.

The four 5-1/2-inch bolts are affixed firmly to hold the cube in place and tightened so that the plywood discs turn true.

The tailstock is backed off and the turning of the pointed tip of the cube is started using a 3/8-inch spindle gouge. The object is to remove the point. **Caution:** Remember to keep hands and fingers from going over the tool rest, as a very nasty laceration will ensue if the spinning bolts are touched.

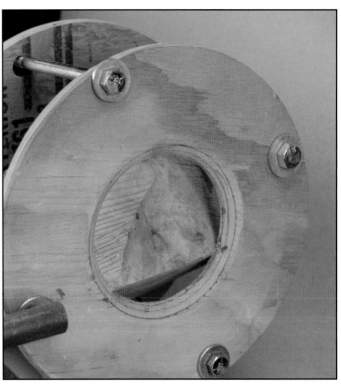

The pyramidal top is removed leaving a triangular concavity.

Use a hand held drill to make a pilot hole for hollowing.

Notice a depth gauge of blue tape is used so the drill doesn't go through the bottom of the block. In calculating the depth, remember that the bottom pyramid of the box will be removed to make the 3 prong foot. This distance must be approximated in the depth of the drilled hole. It is equal to the height of the pyramidal tip that was just removed.

Use the modified 1/2-inch spindle gouge to drill and widen the initial hole. Sweep out to the side as much as possible without making the opening greater than 3/4 inches.

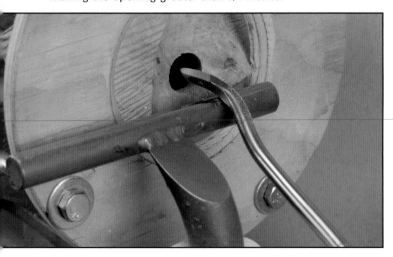

After the limits of the spindle gouge are reached, switch to a small curved hollowing tool to form an interior sphere.

Use a hand-held small Stuart scrapper to smooth the interior of any ridges.

With the rebate tool, cut a 1/8-inch deep, 1/8-inch wide shelf to hold the boxwood disc.

Remove the cube and jig and mount a 1/2-inch thick disc of circular boxwood stock in the O'Donnell jaws.

Turn the proper diameter of both circles to make the fitted disc.

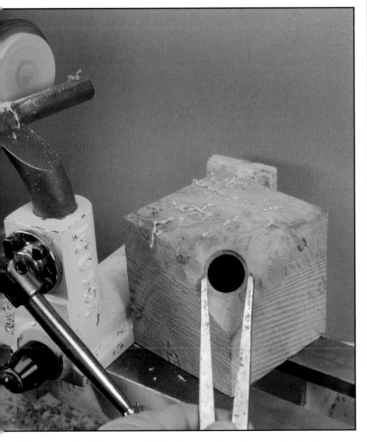

Measure the diameter of the sleeve—interior and exterior openings—and mark them on the boxwood disc.

Turn off the disc and check the fit before remounting the disc in #1 Talon jaws.

Drill a hole in the disc with the 1/2-inch modified spindle gouge, leaving enough boxwood material in the interior for threading. Thread-chase the resulting sleeve—one may see now why the female thread chaser has its tip ground to a taper to fit small openings.

The sleeve is firmly affixed in place. This is the second method of using threads in non-threadable material. It is often utilized to make exotic lids in some woods such as burl, curly maple, or other domestic hardwoods utilized for reliquaries or keepsakes—in those particular instances the sleeve may be used as a chuck to turn a finial top.

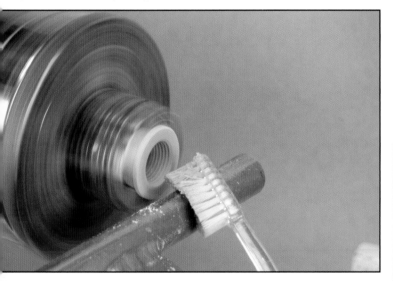

Use some wax on a toothbrush to polish the chased threads of the sleeve.

Turning a contrasting wood for the pyramidal lid is the next step. A rather large piece of stock is needed to cover the distance from one point to the other of the cube's top concavity. A 2-1/2-inch cube of tambootie is selected and mounted in the #3 Talon jaws.

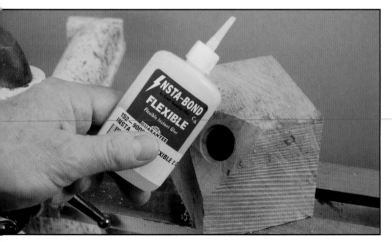

Apply flexible cyanoacrylate to glue the threaded sleeve into the block. Flexible glue is often used to buffer the movement of one timber against the other to prevent cracking of the sleeve.

After measuring slightly proud of the threaded opening of the threaded sleeve turn a spigot about 5/8-inch long, then turn a curvature to the lid base to fit the curvature of the box's top. Place concentric circles at the end of the spigot for a design element.

Use the 20 tpi male chaser to chase threads.

Hold the lid in place to eyeball the curvature, making sure it matches the base.

Check the fit of the threads to make sure the lid fits tightly.

Cut a 1/16-inch deep, 1/16-inch wide stop-gap at the junction of the spigot and lid base with the narrow parting tool.

Make any adjustments in the threads and curvature to tighten the fit. Finish the turned surfaces with sandpaper, steel wool, friction dried lacquer, and then Briwax, buffed lightly. The next step is to cut the three sides of the lid flush on the band saw by pulling the box through. The blade should not touch the sides of the box, but merely cut off the excess material of the lid. Since the box is square it will be easy to cut off excess lid material with three 90 degree rotations.

Next reverse-mount the box in the turning jig, so the top is against the headstock, and tighten the bolts so that the jig turns true.

Turn off the point as was done for the lid area. Finish the turned area by sanding with 150-400 grit waxed sandpaper, #0000 waxed steel wool, diluted lacquer friction dried, and then Briwax.

The rough-turned box is ready to have all six sides sanded with a random orbital hand held sander, using from 150 to 400 grits successively. After the sanding is completed, finish with diluted lacquer and buff with Briwax.

The bottom of the box has a subtle curvature.

The completed box presents an interesting container useful as a keepsake, pet urn, container for placer gold, or cut diamonds smaller than 5 karats.

Chapter 3
Threaded Spherical Boxes on Pedestals Embellished with Rose Engine Ornamental Designs

Spherical boxes are interesting constructions first noted by me many years ago when watching Stuart Batty turn a 3-inch diameter one out of cocobolo at the Provo, Utah, symposium and roll it across the floor to Mike Mahoney to demonstrate its perfect weight and geometry. Since that time I've also noted Christian Delhon turn multi-axis, embellished 4-inch spheres from various exotics at the Provo symposium. Even though both boxes were superb, neither one was threaded for a fit. This chapter will explain the makings of a spherical box with a threaded fitted lid placed on a pedestal, both embellished with ornamental designs from the rose engine lathe.

The first task is selecting the proper timber not only for turning, but for chasing the threads. Spanish olivewood is a beautifully grained wood that can hold threads, especially if a little assistance is applied. The initial procedure is to rough turn a cylinder out of the 3-1/2 x 3-1/2 x 7-inch stock, square the ends with a diamond parting tool, cut a 1/8 inch wide 1-1/2 inch diameter spigot at each end, and then mount the piece in the O'Donnell jaws.

Next, make a hemicircle template for the spherical shape. Using 1/8-inch Plexiglas patterns is a good method of keeping a variety of assorted diameters for turning projects. The template selected is a 3-1/4-inch diameter to allow smoothing out of the hemispheres during construction. First, the cylinder needs to be turned to a perfect diameter of 3-1/4 inches.

Mark a pencil line exactly 3-1/4 inches from the tailstock end, not including the 1/8 inch depth of the spigot. Turn a hemispherical shape leaving a flat portion for mounting in the O'Donnell jaws next to the spigot.

Use the modified 1/2-inch spindle gouge to begin hollowing out the lid. Hollow to a smooth spherical interior surface leaving a wall thickness of 1/4-inch—use of a 2-3/4-inch hemispherical template will help form the interior.

Use the narrow parting tool to part off the lid.

Measure the depth to assure it is 2-3/4 inches.

Remove the base and mount the lid in the O'Donnell jaws. Square the cut surface with the 3/8-inch spindle gouge.

For smoothing the interior, use a round nose scrapper with a negative rake grind.

Smooth the interior holding the scrapper at the demonstrated angle (30 degrees) to prevent catches.

Next use the rebate tool to cut a 1/8-inch wide 1/4-inch deep circular shelf.

With the stop-gap tool cut the stop-gap at the base of the 1/4-inch deep wall to prevent the chaser from fouling on the lid's interior.

Use the 20 tpi female thread chaser to begin chasing threads.

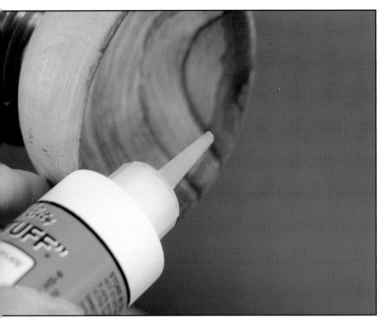

If the threads seem to crumble add cyanoacrylate and let it cure at least 5 minutes. Don't use the cyanoacrylate accelerator or a brittle thread will ensue. (This is the third method of chasing threads in material that ordinarily would not thread.)

Finish the lid using a progression of 150-400 grit waxed sandpaper, reversing directions between grits, #0000 waxed steel wool, friction dried diluted lacquer, and then wax and polish with Briwax. Don't sand the threads but apply the lacquer and Briwax. Remove the lid and remount the base using previously applied pencil mounting marks.

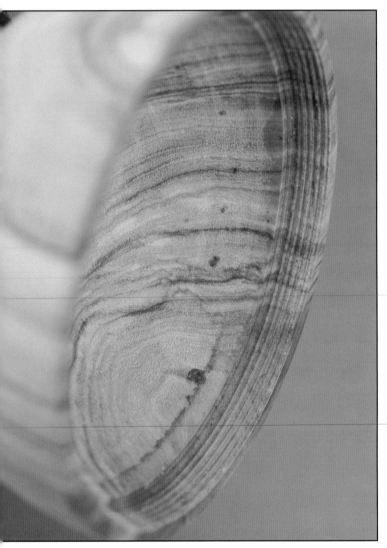

Measure slightly proud of the lid's interior threaded diameter and mark the diameter on the base.

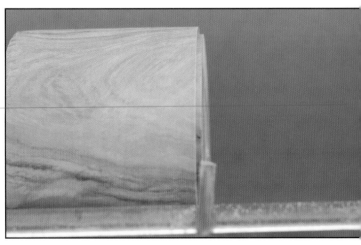

After the glue permeates and cures, finish chasing the threads. If one creates a slight taper interiorly the lid will require only a 90 or 180 degree turn to fit tightly when the box is finished.

Use the rebate tool to cut a narrow spigot to slightly over-fit the lid. Extend the spigot to 1/4-inch wide.

Use the narrow parting tool to cut a 1/16-inch deep 1/16-inch wide stop-gap.

Using the 20 tpi male thread chaser begin to chase the threads. If any crumbling occurs apply cyanoacrylate and let it cure for 5 minutes before rechasing.

Screw on the lid and make any adjustments for a firm fit.

Turn off the lid's spigot and use the template to produce a perfect 3-1/4-inch diameter hemisphere.

Mark a pencil line 3-1/4 inches from the junction of the base and lid.

Begin shaping the base, checking frequently with the template to assure the spherical quality of the box.

After the proper shape is turned remove the lid and set the depth gauge to allow a 1/4-inch thickness at the bottom.

Hollow out the base as was done for the lid using the modified spindle gouge. Check the roundness with the 2-3/4-inch template.

Remove material from the spigot so that the grains match when the lid is tightened. Finish the base's interior and spigot area by sanding with a progression of 150-400 grit waxed sandpaper, #0000 waxed steel wool, friction dried diluted lacquer, and then polish with Briwax. Don't sand the threads.

Finish the exterior of the sphere as was done for the interior in preparation of applying the embellishments with the rose engine lathe.

The Rose Engine Lathe

A point of digression is needed here to describe the rose engine lathe. Personally, I had no idea what a rose engine lathe was until attending a seminar at the Portland AAW Symposium in June 2007. Jon McGill gave an excellent series of lectures on its history, construction, and use. An article he wrote can be found on the AAW's web site if one clicks on American Woodturner (the Association's official quarterly journal) and scrolls down to rose engine lathe. There is also an ornamental wood turning web site to peruse—ornamentalturning.org.

A rose engine lathe is an ornamental lathe. The term rose engine comes from the fact that the produced face plate patterns appear like the petals of a rose. Ornamental lathe work dates back to the 1600s. Some of the most famous lathes were designed and produced by Holtzapffel and are usually found in museums. They may have price tags in the hundred of thousands. Less expensive ornamental lathes ($40,000) can sometimes be found to do ornamental work.

Most of the ornamental designs were done in metal, such as watch cases or jewelry boxes. During the Victorian era many intricate pieces were produced from ivory. Today, only a few gifted ornamental turners create lovely detailed intricate gallery pieces, but interest by both turners and consumers is increasing.

The idea of the rose engine lathe is to have a high speed cutter with high speed steel tips cutting fine designs in rather dense timbers as they slowly rotate. The designs may be placed in a face plate fashion or a spindle fashion by moving the cutter to and fro. The cutter system is mounted on an adjustable X-Y axis table which looks like part of a milling machine. The lathe's shaft is mounted in a rockable head stock with plastic patterned discs at the distal end. The particular lathe utilized for this book allows the use of 2 discs simultaneously with adjustable rubbers to transmit the patterns. The rubbers are held in contact with the patterned discs by elastic tubing. A motor drive unit with step down pulleys allows the rotation to be 10 rpms while the cutter drive unit turns at 10,000 rpms (like a router) cutting the patterns. The many plastic discs (9 for the described unit) may be mounted at different tilts (9 to 18 combinations) yielding over 2 million possibilities of design elements.

The construction of the lathe as per Jon McGill's kit requires a bit more than casual experience in woodworking. A few modifications are necessary to custom fit various changes and the use of Baltic birch instead of MDF allows a lighter box and much nicer material with which to work. Applying a darker finish helps hide some of the blackwood and other darker dusts during use.

Although the lathe is heavy, it is still portable. The X-Y axis table is bolted on and may be moved for larger pieces or lathe transport. The maximum diameter for this design is 12 inches and the maximum length with the X-Y axis table moved back depends on how adept the turner is at firmly affixing the extended stock. Obviously no tailstock is used for support as the headstock rocks.

A view of the cutting end of the lathe shows the X-Y axis table with the cutter mounted on a moveable post. The 1/8-inch diameter urethane drive belt often breaks so that extra belts are necessary—an easy solution is to make up several and keep them on hand. A standard Oneway Talon chuck is used to mount the stock.

Above: The back side view shows 2 rose engine plastic discs mounted with the rubbers retracted. The 1/4-inch diameter custom-made urethane belts on the step-down pulleys are noted in orange.

Below: The side view shows the 1/25 hp drive motor and the rocking headstock.

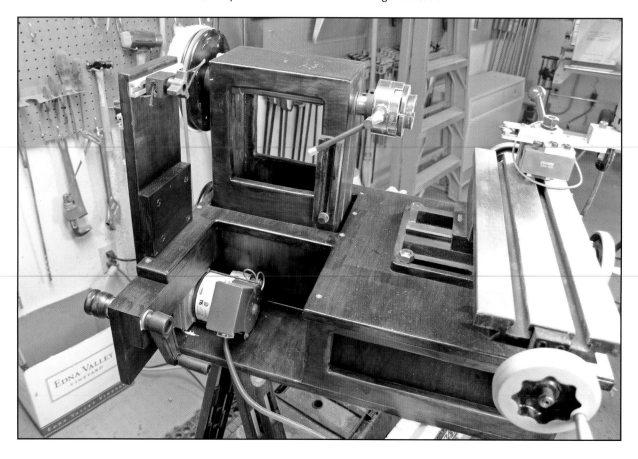

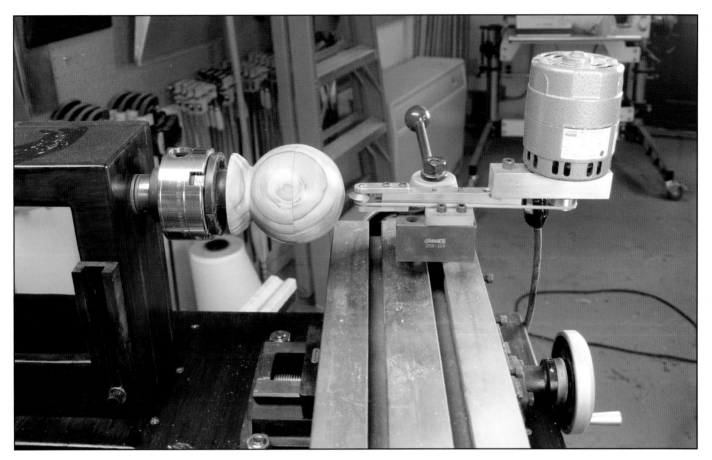

The spherical box is mounted in the Talon chuck using #3 jaws, with the cutter brought up to but not touching the stock. The drive motor is turned on to start the rocking pattern and then the cutter is turned on and brought up to lightly touch and cut the sphere.

The 5-star rose pattern cut in the wood is partially complete.

Continue to cut further patterns after repositioning the cutter.

Remove the lid and cut another pattern on the interior of the bottom.

Remove the base from the Talon chuck and make a threaded or friction fitted mount out of scrap stock.

Turn the base to a perfect 3-1/4 inch diameter hemisphere. Sand to completion and apply finishes as was done for other parts of the sphere.

The finished base interior next to an embellished pedestal holder.

The completed spherical box on its decorative pedestal presents a unique piece.

Chapter 4
Threaded Rotating Ring Capsule Boxes with Rose Engine Lathe Decorations

Many years ago I learned how to make rotating ring boxes from Hans Weissflog and thought of new approaches to utilize the techniques. Instead of using blackwood with some of the sapwood incorporated into the piece the wild patterns of black and white ebony are employed to accent rings then the rose engine lathe used to embellish the capsule box. Although black and white ebony is not the best timber to turn or use to chase threads, cyanoacrylate is most helpful in bridging the working gap.

Turn 3-inch cubed black and white ebony to a cylinder between centers, square the ends with the diamond parting tool, and then form 1/8-inch deep, 1-1/2-inch diameter spigots at each end to fit the O'Donnell jaws. Mark a pencil line 1-1/8-inch from the tailstock end.

Begin to round over the lid to its spigot, leaving a flat surface to rest against the O'Donnell jaws.

Use the narrow parting tool to cut a defining slot for parting.

Part off the lid.

Remove the base and chuck up the lid. Use the 1/2-inch skew to square the cut surface.

Use the modified spindle gouge to hollow out the lid.

Check for the proper depth.

Set the depth gauge to leave a wall thickness 3/16-inch when hollowing the interior of the lid.

Use a round-nose scraper to smooth out the interior.

Use the rebate tool to cut a 3/32-inch wide, 1/4-inch deep rebate.

Use the stop-gap tool to cut a stop-gap at the end of the rebate.

Use the 20 tpi female thread chaser to start the threads.

Apply cyanoacrylate, letting it permeate the wood and cure for about 5 minutes. Finish chasing the threads.

Mark a ring with dividers on the interior of the lid. Leave the dividers at this setting and put them aside to mark an exterior ring on the lid later.

With a second set of dividers, mark another, wider ring on the interior of the lid and set those dividers aside, as well, to mark the same size ring on the exterior lid later.

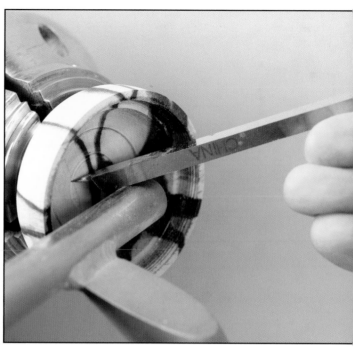

Begin to carefully cut at a 30 degree angle along the first marked ring. After a similar cut is made on the other or exterior side a free disc will be created able to rotate in the created grove.

Use a custom ground high speed steel tool to form a knife point about .5 mm thick and 3/8 inches long.

Cut in to a depth of 3/4 of the knife's length.

Notice the side view and thickness of the cutting point.

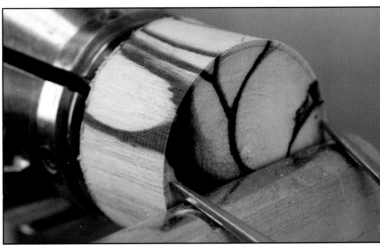

Remove the lid and remount the base using the previously applied pencil mounting marks. Using dividers, mark slightly proud of the lid's opening on the skew-squared surface of the base.

Do the same for the second ring. A similar cut on the exterior side will free up a rotating ring able to rotate in the created grove.

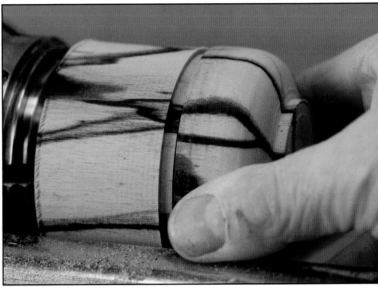

Cut a slight spigot to the marked line. Check the fit to make sure it is still proud of the threaded opening of the lid.

Finish the lid's interior by sanding and applying finishes as was done for the other boxes. Don't sand the threads.

Extend the spigot to 1/4 inch, then cut a 1/16-inch deep, 1/16-inch wide stop-gap for thread-chasing.

Begin chasing threads with the male thread-chaser.

Apply cyanoacrylate on the crumbled threads and let it cure for about 5 minutes. Re-chase the threads.

Check the fit to make sure it is tight.

Hollow out the base to a wall thickness of 3/16-inch.

Smooth out the interior surface with the round nose scrapper. When sharpening the scrapper remember to take off the burr with a diamond card.

Finish by sanding and apply the finishes. Don't sand the threads.

Use the ring diameters from the inside to mark the same diameters on the lid. Dividers or calipers may be used.

Replace the lid and turn off the spigot.

Finish sanding with 150-400 waxed sandpaper reversing directions between grits, #0000 waxed steel wool, friction dried diluted lacquer, and then polish with Briwax.

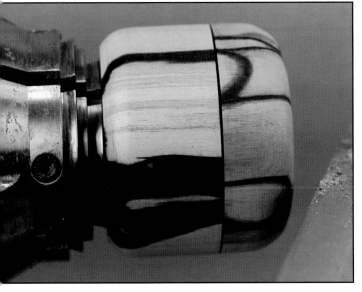

Check to make sure the tight fitting lid's pattern matches the base. If not remove some material from the base's spigot until the patterns coincide.

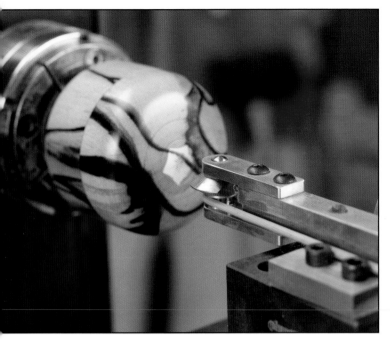

Mount the box by its base's spigot in the Talon chuck and apply a central design with the rose engine lathe. Be sure to cut a pattern that lies within the boundaries of the ring (central disc).

Apply another design outside of the second ring.

Remove the lid and apply a design to the interior of the box.

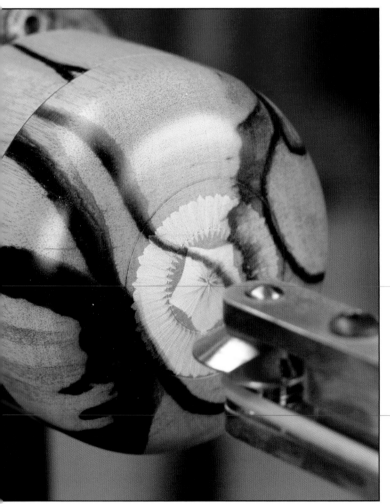

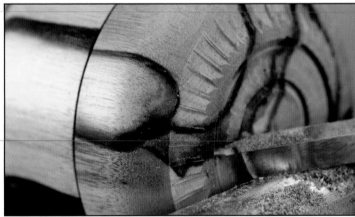

Apply a different design between the rings.

Remove the base and screw the box together. Place it in the O'Donnell jaws and cut at a 30 degree angle along the inner ring to a depth of 3/4 the needle knife blade to create a rotating central disc. On the second outer mark make the same type cut to create a rotating ring. The two cuts give a rotating disc and rotating ring.

Make a screw chuck to mount the base and turn off the spigot and finish as was done for the other surfaces.

Use the screw chuck mount in the Talon jaws on the rose engine lathe and cut another design on the bottom of the box. After cuts are made apply diluted lacquer to the cut surfaces then polish with Briwax for a pleasant appearance.

The bottom and top exteriors of the rotating ringed capsule box.

Note the finished interior of lid and base of the rotating ringed capsule box.

The completed rotating ringed rose engine embellished capsule box with grains matching is another unique piece.

Chapter 5
The Nuts and Bolts of Threaded Boxes

I remember seeing one of Allan Batty's famous nut and bolt boxes made out of boxwood on display several years ago. Not long ago, Petter Herud revised the method and made quite a few out of various exotics. The idea is most clever as well as unusual, so with the use of the rose engine lathe another twist may be added to the process.

The idea of a bolt box is to have a container that appears to be what it isn't, that is a box to hold something. One of the problems in construction is forming the long narrow channel for the box.

Using an 11/16-inch diameter Boeing surplus aircraft drill bit to drill a 3- or 4-inch deep hole solves the problem of construction. The bits are sold at the Boeing surplus warehouse on Wednesdays and are marked down to $5/lb. Once upon a time I purchased two handfuls of different sizes. The bit has 2 lumens used to pump oil as a lubricant and cooling agent. I had a number 3 Morse taper with a side connection for compressed air fashioned at the local machine shop and also had the taper tapped to fit the threaded bit. Instead of oil as a cooling agent I use compressed air. It also removes dust and debris from the drilled hole. If one doesn't have access to Boeing Surplus then use a sharp Forstner drill bit of the desired diameter.

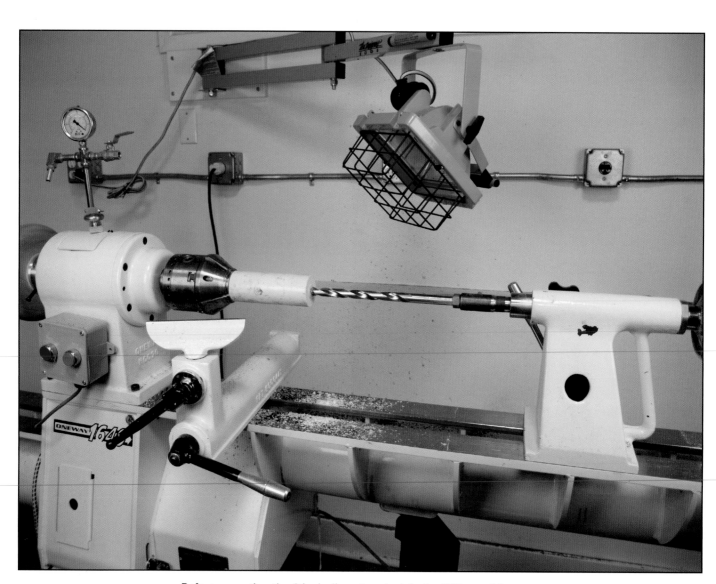

Before mounting the 2 inch diameter stock in the O'Donnell jaws
be sure to square the ends with a parting tool between centers.

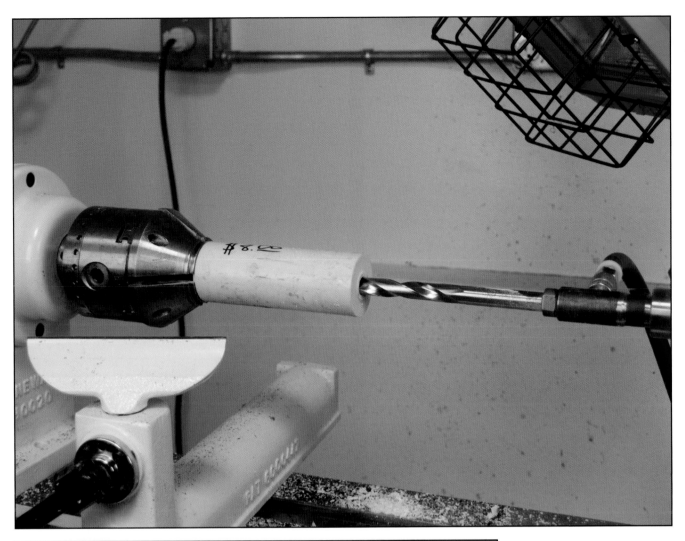

Above: An important concept when drilling wood or imitation ivory—a plastic like substance—is to take one's time. Drill in at 1 or 1/2 mm per turn of the tailstock handle. Have the emergency on-off switch at knee level so that it may be hit immediately upon having a catch—the compressed air hose will quickly wrap around the bit's base. Drill at 100 to 200 rpms only. Support the air hose connection with a gloved left hand to prevent the bit from spinning around.

Left: A nice smooth opening 3-1/2 inches deep is drilled in the synthetic substance without creating any cracks or chips.

Place a live center in the tailstock and re-square the end.

Mark a circumferential pencil line 1/4 inch to the left (towards the headstock) of the depth mark.

Check the depth of the drill hole.

Use the diamond parting tool to cut 1/4 inch deep along the pencil line. Keep the lathe speed at 3500 rpms.

Transfer the depth to the the outside and mark.

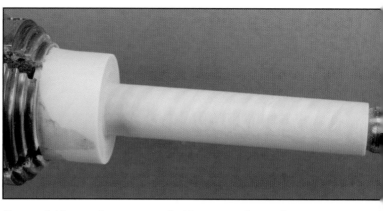

On careful inspection very small chip-out marks can be seen.

Use the roughing gouge to reduce the diameter of the material. A scrapping cut at high speed—3500 rpms—is most effective in removing material and preventing chipping of the semi-crystallized substance.

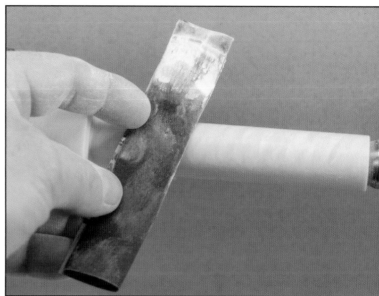

Sand the surface with a progression of 100-400 grit sand paper to remove chip marks.

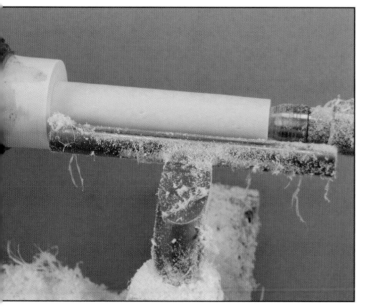

The tube of the box has been reduced to a wall thickness of 1/8 inch.

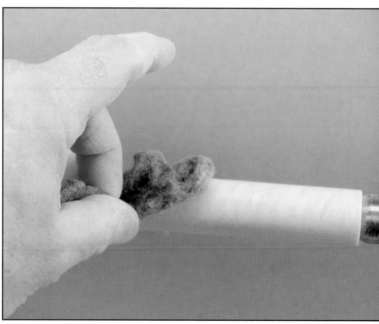

Buff with #0000 steel wool to a glossy finish.

Use the narrow parting tool to cut a 1/32 inch deep, 1/16 inch wide stop-gap 1/4 inch from the tailstock end in preparation for thread-chasing.

The live center prevents close contact with the synthetic tube so a narrow tapered metal tube is used to back off the live center and allow the chaser proximity to the synthetic tube's end. If one tries to thread chase without tailstock support an incomplete thread will ensue.

Close-up inspection shows no chipping so it is ready for thread chasing.

Use the 18 tpi male chaser to create the threads. Remember to pull away from the tube upon reaching the stop-gap and chase at 200 rpms.

Part off the tube with the narrow parting tool after backing off the tailstock. Make sure to catch the parted tube with the free hand.

Mount another 2 inch diameter synthetic ivory stock between centers and square the ends. Mount the stock in the O'Donnell jaws and bring up the tailstock. Use a skew as a scrapper to round the cylinder while turning at 3500 rpms—this material scrapes much better than it turns. Using the narrow parting tool, cut a disc as wide as the exact thickness of the hollow tube. Cut another disc about 5/32 for a washer and a third disc the width of the first.

Measure with calipers slightly proud of the synthetic tube's diameter and mark it on the thin disc.

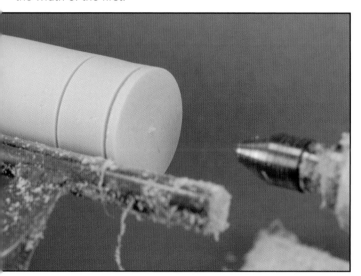

Part off the first disc after backing off the tailstock.

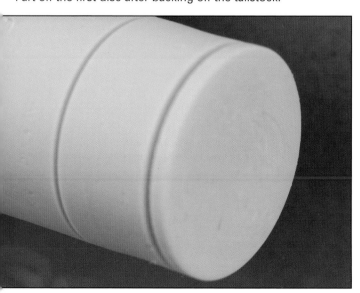

Scrape the revealed surface of the second disc at high speeds with the skew chisel.

Use the modified hollowing tool to open the center.

Use the rebate tool to scrape to the marked line.

Sand with 100-400 grit sandpaper and polish with #0000 steel wool.

Part off the disc and set it aside with the first parted disc.

Measure slightly shy of the hollow tube's diameter.

Center that measurement on the next disc.

Hollow out the disc to the depth of parting cut.

Re-chuck the thin, washer disc with the finished side facing the headstock.

Use the rebate tool to scrape square the cut surface being careful not to enlarge the opening. Part off the disc and remove the stock from the chuck.

Remove material to meet the opening from the other side. Sand to completion and buff with steel wool.

Use a pencil to make the 6 marks.

Remove the finished washer and remount the first parted-off disc in the O'Donnell jaws. Use the 1/2 inch skew in a scrapping fashion to create a convex smooth surface. Sand the surface to completion and then buff with #0000 steel wool.

Use a straight edge to connect the marks. On the synthetic ivory the material will be sanded off. On wood it may be cut off on a band saw (1/8 inch blade, 12 tpi) and then sanded.

Notice the index numbers on the headstock. The bolt will have six sides so that on a 24 point index a mark needs to be made at 4, 8, 12, 16, 20, & 24.

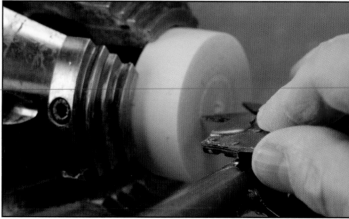

Reverse mount the disc. Measure slightly shy of the thread-chased end of the tube, and center that measurement on the disc.

Hollow the center to a depth of 3/8-inch, but just to the mark.

Place a stop-gap at the end of the hollowing to prevent fouling of the thread chaser. Sand to completion and buff with steel wool.

Use the 18 tpi female thread chaser to create a firm fit for the tube. Chase at 300 rpms.

Screw in the tube and bring up the tailstock. Note: The tube should be centered if the threads were chased exactly. If the tube is not centered, unscrew it and try to center it as it is re-screwed into the lid.

Begin to chase threads (200 rpms) from the tailstock end of the tube inwards.

Chase the threads to a width of 1-1/4 inches.

Support the tube with the left hand and cut a taper and flat surface after turning up the speed (2000 rpms).

Remove the lid and tube, and then remount the last disc. Sand the surface smooth then buff with steel wool. As before, use the indexer to mark 6 equidistant points and connect them with pencil lines.

Reverse mount the disc then sand and buff the other side.

Use the 18 tpi female thread chaser at 300 rpms to chase threads the entire interior width of the disc.

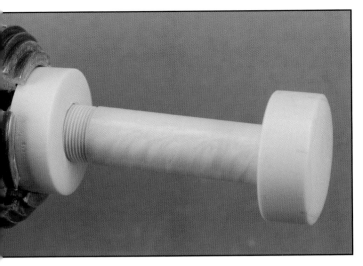

Check the fit for the tube then remove the disc from the chuck.

Use a coarse belt sander to squarely sand off the 6 marked sides of the disc.

Mount the lid in the #3 Talon jaws on the rose engine lathe then bring up the cutter.

The completed nut is ready to be sanded to completion.

Turn on the lathe and then turn on the cutter to carefully begin cutting the desired pattern in the lid.

Sand off the 6 marked sides of the lid with the coarse belt sander.

A careful, gentle touch is necessary during finer sanding.

The completed bolt lid is ready to be sanded to completion.

The sanded and buffed pieces are ready to be assembled.

The completed bolt box with washer and nut decorated with the rose engine embellishment on its lid is truly unique.

Chapter 6
Threaded Pierced-Through Boxes with Rose Engine Lathe Embellishments

Pierced-through lidded boxes are another invention of Hans Weissflog. I first learned how to construct them from Hans in a class many years ago and have since added personal interpretation and changes to establish an altered technique. Most of the pierced-through processes are accomplished on cross grain timber. When making a box with a threaded lid, an end grain stock chases better, with less fractured threads. The problem is easily solved by making pierced-through discs out of cross grain timber and gluing them into the lids of end grain boxes. Using differing timbers as to color also adds more embellishments, as well as applying the rose engine lathe technique. Some synthetics also work well in the pierced-through process.

After selecting cocobolo—2-1/2-inch square stock, 3 inches long—cut it to a near cylinder on a band saw, turn it to a cylinder between centers, square the ends, and then turn 2mm spigots on each end to fit the 2-inch O'Donnell jaws. Mount the stock in the O'Donnell jaws and true the cylinder. Mark the mounting point on the stock for future reference.

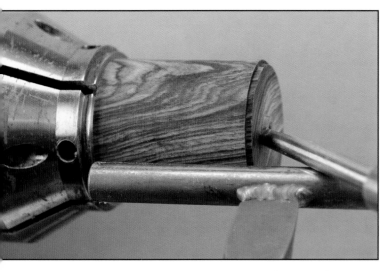

Use a 3/8-inch spindle gouge to smooth the tailstock surface area.

Remove the base and mount the lid in the O'Donnell jaws. The top of the lid is in the headstock. A narrow spigot—2mm—is used for mounting. It will later be turned off; a thick spigot would create problems gluing in the finished, pierced-through disc for finishing. Use the modified spindle gouge to hollow out the lid.

Use a rule to measure the lid area. Once again, the golden mean will be utilized. I like to use a metric rule with the smaller measurements. Millimeters are easier to read than thousandths of an inch. The lid will be 16 mm, which means the base should be 24 mm after the distance for the threaded spigot and stop-gap is added on. Mark the measurement with a pencil.

Part off the lid with the narrow parting tool.

Measure the depth to allow an interior shelf of 2 mm.

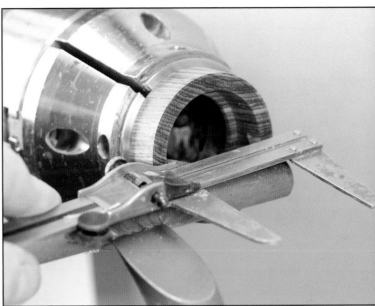

Check with calipers to assure the wall is square and then sand to completion.

Use the rebate tool to square the interior sides of the wall.

Use the stop-gap tool to cut a stop-gap 4 mm in from the edge.

Open the top of the lid, leaving a 2-3 mm shelf for mounting the pierced-through disc.

With a female 18 tpi thread chaser begin to chase threads.

After the threads are chased polish with a wax coated toothbrush.

Extend the spigot to 4 mm and use the narrow parting tool to cut the stop-gap.

Remove the lid and remount the base aligning to the pencil mounting marks. Measure slightly proud of the lid's opening and mark it on the base. Use a diamond parting tool to cut a slight spigot to the mark.

With the male 18 tpi chaser begin to cut threads pulling back when the stop-gap is reached.

Hold the lid to the spigot to make sure the fit is snug.

Check the fit of the lid. Make any necessary adjustments so that the grain lines up when the lid is tight. Cut a 1 mm deep, 1.5 mm wide defining mark on the base.

Measure 24 mm from the stop-gap area and make a pencil mark.

Use the narrow parting tool to cut in about 4 mm to define the base.

Use the modified spindle gouge to hollow out the base. The bottom thickness should be about 5 mm because rose engine designs will be cut on both inside and outside of the base bottom.

Use a round-nose scrapper to smooth the interior. Hint: After sharpening a scrapper, remember to take off the burr to prevent catches.

Mount the base in the Talon chuck on the rose engine lathe and cut a design on the interior base bottom.

Approach the base at a 30 degree angle.

Sand to completion and use waxed #0000 steel wool.

Above: Making the pierced-through disc is a rather simple process. If one uses contrasting woods, such as blackwood with holly (left), blackwood with imitation ivory (center), or blackwood wood with boxwood, interesting contrasts may be had when one peers through the openings. Remember to use cross grain so that the narrow rings don't fracture and fall out. The imitation ivory often is difficult to turn, especially if the piece is slightly crystallized. It is, however, what we will use in this demonstration.

The best approach is to cut out discs with the band saw then turn them true using the O'Donnell jaws—remember the imitation ivory scrapes better than it turns. The pieces should be about 5 or 6 mm thick to allow easy mounting and handling. After the two parts are squared they are glued together using flexible cyanoacrylate. The flexible glue has a little give when turning, as opposed to the regular set crystallized superglue.

Cut the blackwood down to the mark.

Mount the imitation ivory side in the jaws and then use dividers to mark a centered diameter slightly smaller than the diameter of the opening at the bottom of the lid.

Check the fit on the lid.

Check the fit in the lid's top opening to assure that it is snug.

Reverse the stock and measure the top opening of the lid. Scrape the edge of the lighter material reducing its diameter to the mark.

Use a straight skew to scrape the lighter surface to a thickness of 1.5 mm.

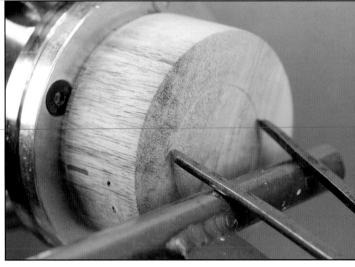

Next mount a cylindrical waste block in the Axminster eccentric chuck in the central position. Use at least 2 mounting screws.

Mark the diameter of the blackwood disc on the waste block and cut a 3 mm deep receptacle.

On the back of the face plate, mark mounting positions 1, 2, and 3. Mark the same numbers on the bottom of the waste cylinder for future reference.

Check to make sure the fit is tight with no free play.

Remove the face plate, then reattach it, putting the #3 position in the center, and the center at the #3 position, to give an off-centered mount.

Use hot melt glue to hold the disc in place.

Replace the chuck and plate on the lathe and hand rotate the stock to draw a guiding pencil mark for the cut ring location.

Remove the chuck and screws on the face plate. Place the center hole in #2 screw hole and the #2 hole at the center to give the second rotation. Draw in the pencil guide line by hand rotation.

Use a piece of high speed steel ground down to form a 1 mm by 1 mm sharpened cutter. The side view is noted with a 40 degree angled cutting tip.

The top view of the cutter is demonstrated here.

Remove the chuck and screws on the face plate. Place the center hole in #1 screw hole and the #1 hole at the center to give the third rotation. Draw in the pencil guide line by hand rotation.

Turning at 800 rpms carefully push in the cutter into the pencil line until the blackwood is reached.

Move over 1 mm and make another cut. Do the same again until the edge is reached leaving 6 circular grooves.

Change the position of the face plate as before, to the next 120 degree rotation, and cut the second semi-circular pattern.

Move the stock to the next 120 degree rotation and cut the third semi-circular pattern.

Use the narrow parting tool to part off the blackwood leaving a thickness of 2 to 3 mm.

Mount the imitation ivory portion in the O'Donnell jaws.

Cut or scrape the blackwood down to 1.5 mm thickness.

Use the 1 mm cutter to cut 1 mm wide, 1.5 mm deep concentric circles in the black wood until they reach the imitation ivory.

A close-up shows the pierced-through effect displaying the black-on-white pattern.

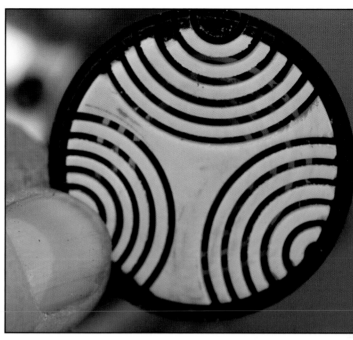

The reverse shows white-on-black. The fine threads of material may be removed using a cross-stitch needle.

The completed disc may be glued (flexible cyanoacrylate) into the lid and then the rim turned down to the disc. Finish rounding over the edges.

Sand to completion after rounding the base.

Part off the base and reverse mount it on a jam chuck to finish the bottom.

The inside of the finished base and lid display interesting patterns.

Sand to completion before mounting it on the rose engine lathe.

Mount the base on the rose engine lathe and cut a design on the bottom. Apply diluted lacquer to the cut surfaces both inside and outside the base.

The completed pierced-though box is another interesting art object.

Chapter 7
Gallery

Four cubic boxes with threaded pyramidal lids: back row; maple burl with tambootie, zebrawood with cocobolo; front row; figured myrtle with madrone burl, African mahogany with pink ivory.

Top box: Cocobolo spherical box on imitation ivory pedestal. Opened spherical box of cocobolo with rose engine embellishments; imitation ivory pedestal with ornamental designs. **Middle Box:** Spalted boxwood spherical box on pink ivory pedestal. Opened spherical box of spalted boxwood with rose engine embellishments; pink ivory pedestal with ornamental designs. **Bottom Box:** Opened spherical box of violet rosewood with rose engine embellishments; synthetic tortoise shell pedestal with ornamental designs. Violet rosewood spherical box on imitation tortoise shell pedestal.

Above: Collection of spherical boxes on pedestals: left to right; Olivewood on bubinga, cocobolo on imitation ivory, spalted boxwood on pink ivory, English hawthorn on violet rosewood, violet rosewood on imitation tortoise shell.

Right: Opened spherical box of English hawthorn with rose engine embellishments; violet rosewood pedestal with ornamental designs.

English hawthorn spherical box with rose engine
embellishments on violet rosewood ornamental pedestal.

Above: Collection of cylinder boxes constructed out of left over cut-offs from a peppermill project. All threads are chased in dyed epoxy.

Opposite (clockwise from top left): Opened rotating ringed boxes of black and white ebony showing rose engine design of interior base.

Top and bottom of rotating ringed boxes showing rose engine lathe design.

Completed rotating ringed boxes of black and white ebony.

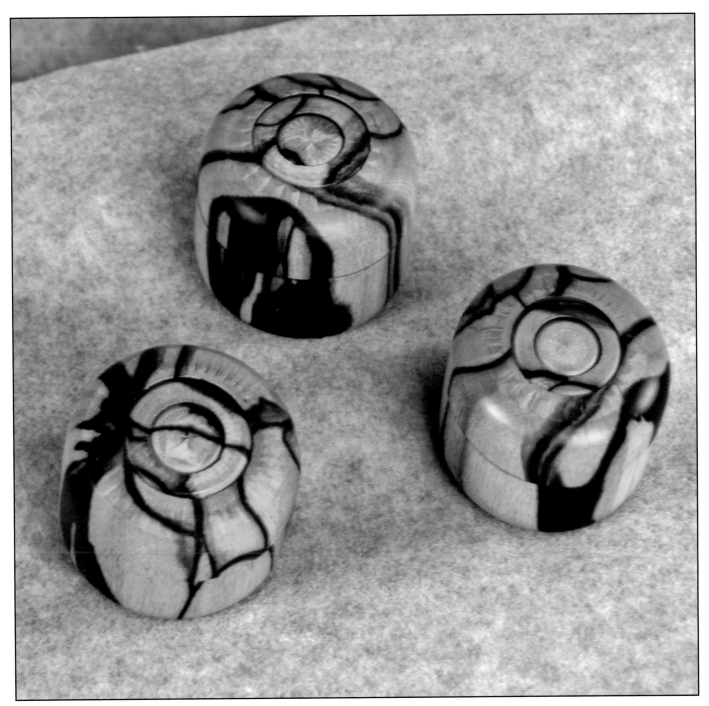

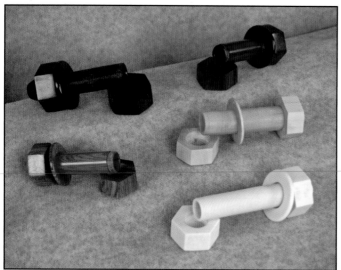

Top: Collection of bolt boxes showing ornamental designs; (clockwise), violet rosewood, boxwood, imitation ivory, tulipwood, kingwood, blackwood, imitation ivory, cocobolo, and pink ivory.

Middle Left: Opened bolt boxes (clockwise) of cocobolo, blackwood, violet rosewood, boxwood, and imitation ivory.

Middle Right: Closed bolt boxes showing ornamental designs on lids; (clockwise from far left) cocobolo, boxwood, violet rosewood, blackwood, and imitation ivory.

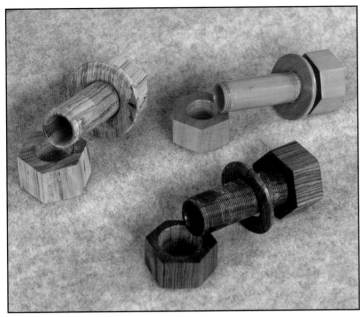

Clockwise from top left: Bolt boxes of tulipwood, kingwood, and pink ivory.

Bolt boxes of kingwood, tulipwood, and pink ivory showing rose engine design of lids.

Collection of bolt boxes showing ornamental designs.

Above: Grouping of boxes with blackwood and boxwood bottle top tapered threaded finials. Back row; redwood burl; second row, bocote; front row, bloodwood.

Right: Collection of tambootie, madrone burl, Australian lacewood, and blackwood boxes.

Above: Collection of hollow form curly maple boxes with blackwood bottle top, tapered threaded finials fit into boxwood sleeves. Such boxes are useful as keepsakes, pet urns, or utilitarian containers.

Left: Collection of figured myrtle boxes with blackwood bottle top tapered threaded finials fit into boxwood sleeves.

Above: Tops of 2 capsule and 1 cylinder threaded boxes with dyed rose engine designs.
Below: Bottoms of 2 capsule and 1 cylinder threaded boxes with dyed rose engine designs.

Clockwise from top left: Spalted boxwood capsule box and cocobolo cylinder box, both with subtle rose engine design on their lids.

Three completed pierced-through lidded boxes.

Interior of blackwood and cocobolo pierced-through lidded boxes. Notice the lace pattern of the lids and rose engine lathe designs of the base interior.

Finished blackwood pierced-through lidded box showing the fine lace-like pattern. The inset pierced-through timber is boxwood end grain turned on 2 different axes.

Acknowledgements

It is most important to acknowledge and thank those particular turners who first theorized specific box constructions, techniques, and problem solving in producing many of the box types described in the text.

Petter Herud with his ingenious gift of artistic expressions is credited with using dyed epoxy for thread-chasing in non-threadable timbers as well as creating cleverly constructed threaded bolt boxes.

Credit also goes to **Allan Batty** who showed both of us how to make bolt boxes as well as hand thread-chase.

Clead Christiansen is credited with making a jig to hold and then produce a cubic hollowed out box.

Stuart Batty and **Christian Delhon** are credited with conceptualizing decorated spherical boxes on pedestals.

Hans Weissflog deserves the credit for inventing rotating ringed boxes as well as pierced-through lidded boxes.

To all those master turners I say thank you for the opportunity to watch as well as learn their techniques. It is only through the generosity of gifted instructors we all learn and improve so that not only may we produce lovely gallery pieces but also teach and inspire others to try their hand at additional signature steps.

I should also like to thank Doug Congdon-Martin for his untiring editing of text and photos; his most able and experienced staff for photo layouts and photography selection, and last but not least Peter and Pete Schiffer for their support and encouragement as well as expertise in publishing and marketing.